The
First Four
Books
of Poems

LOUISE GLÜCK

The
First Four
Books
of Poems

Firstborn

The House on Marshland

Descending Figure

The Triumph of Achilles

THE ECCO PRESS

THE ECCO PRESS
100 West Broad Street
Hopewell, New Jersey 08525
Published simultaneously in Canada by
Penguin Books Canada Ltd., Ontario
Printed in the United States of America

First Edition

Some of the poems in this work have originally appeared in the following
publications: *Antaeus; American Poetry Review; The Atlantic Monthly; Book
Week; Equal Time; The Goddard Journal; Gulf Stream; Iowa Review;
Lillabulero; Mademoiselle; The Nation; New American Review; New Measure;
The New Republic; The New Yorker; Pequod; Poetry; Salmagundi; Solstice;
12 Poets; Tri-Quarterly; Water Table; Yale Review.*

Library of Congress Cataloging-in-Publication Data
Glück, Louise
[Poems. Selections]
The first four books of poems / Louise Glück.
p. cm.
ISBN 0-88001-421-0
I. Title.
PS3557.L8A6 1995
811'.54—dc20   94-43656

The text of this book is set in Bembo

TO DAN

CONTENTS

FIRSTBORN (1968)

I THE EGG

The Chicago Train   5
The Egg   6
Thanksgiving   9
Hesitate to Call   10
My Cousin in April   11
Returning a Lost Child   12
Labor Day   13
The Wound   14
Silverpoint   16
Early December in Croton-on-Hudson   17

II THE EDGE

The Edge   21
Grandmother in the Garden   22
Pictures of the People in the War   23
The Racer's Widow   24
Portrait of the Queen in Tears   25
Bridal Piece   26
My Neighbor in the Mirror   27
My Life before Dawn   28
The Lady in the Single   29
The Cripple in the Subway   30
Nurse's Song   31
Seconds   32
Letter from Our Man in Blossomtime   33

The Cell   34

The Islander   35

Letter from Provence   36

Memo from the Cave   37

Firstborn   38

La Force   39

The Game   40

III COTTONMOUTH COUNTRY

Cottonmouth Country   43

Phenomenal Survivals of Death in Nantucket   44

Easter Season   46

Scraps   47

The Tree House   48

Meridian   49

Late Snow   50

To Florida   51

The Slave Ship   52

Solstice   53

The Inlet   54

Saturnalia   55

THE HOUSE ON MARSHLAND (1975)

I ALL HALLOWS

All Hallows   61

The Pond   62

Gretel in Darkness   63

For My Mother   64

Archipelago   65

The Magi   66

The Shad-blow Tree   67

Messengers   68

The Murderess   69

Flowering Plum   70

Nativity Poem   71

To Autumn   72

Still Life   73

For Jane Myers   74

Gratitude   75

Poem   76

The School Children   77

Jeanne d'Arc   78

Departure   79

Gemini   80

II THE APPLE TREES

The Undertaking   83

Pomegranate   84

Brennende Liebe   86

Abishag   87

12. 6. 71   89

Love Poem   90

Northwood Path   91

The Fire   92

The Fortress   93

Here Are My Black Clothes   94

Under Taurus   95

The Swimmer   96

The Letters   97

Japonica   98

The Apple Trees   99

DESCENDING FIGURE (1980)

I THE GARDEN

The Drowned Children   105

The Garden   106

Palais des Arts   111
Pietà   112
Descending Figure   113
Thanksgiving   116

II THE MIRROR
Epithalamium   119
Illuminations   120
The Mirror   121
Portrait   122
Tango   123
Swans   126
Night Piece   127
Portland, 1968   128
Porcelain Bowl   129
Dedication to Hunger   130
Happiness   135

III LAMENTATIONS
Autumnal   139
Aubade   140
Aphrodite   141
Rosy   142
The Dream of Mourning   143
The Gift   144
World Breaking Apart   145
The Return   146
Lamentations   147

THE TRIUMPH OF ACHILLES (1985)

I

Mock Orange   155
Metamorphosis   156

Brooding Likeness   159

Exile   160

Winter Morning   161

Seated Figure   164

Mythic Fragment   165

Hyacinth   166

The Triumph of Achilles   168

Baskets   169

Liberation   172

II

The Embrace   175

Marathon   176

Summer   186

III

The Reproach   189

The End of the World   191

The Mountain   194

A Parable   195

Day Without Night   197

Elms   201

Adult Grief   202

Hawk's Shadow   203

From the Japanese   204

Legend   209

Morning   211

Horse   212

INDEX OF POEMS   213

AUTHOR'S NOTE

The books contained here haven't been changed, which doesn't mean the poems couldn't be improved. But the idea of revising old work seems odd to me, the spirit animating that work being no longer accessible. Some of the poems, chiefly those in *Firstborn*, might, in being reconstructed, evaporate; to have culled radically would dictate another form. And the idea of selected poems alarms me; I cannot rid myself of attaching to that enterprise a valedictory taint.

Toward the poems of *Firstborn*, some written nearly 35 years ago, I try to cultivate an attitude of embarrassed tenderness. And the books that followed grew out of it, in that each tried to respond to what I perceived as too-defining limitations. After *Firstborn*, I set myself the task of making poems as single sentences, having found myself trapped in fragments. After *The House on Marshland*, I tried to wean myself from conspicuous syntactical quirks and a recurring vocabulary—what begins as vision degenerates into mannerism. And after *Descending Figure*, my favorite of the books here, I tried to learn to use questions and contractions, because I finally noticed that I'd refused them and it seemed interesting to discover how the poems would sound if I didn't: interesting and personally illuminating, in that I was forced to recognize how purposefully I had insisted on distance.

The other reason for presenting these books intact is formal: much thought went into their shaping. And to this extent, I regret their being fused (though no publisher can keep so many things in print in separate editions indefinitely). I felt, even before I learned to read, that a book was a holy object; this awe perpetuates itself in each attempt to make, of a pile of poems, a speaking whole.

The
First Four
Books
of Poems

Firstborn
(1968)

I

The Egg

THE CHICAGO TRAIN

Across from me the whole ride
Hardly stirred: just Mister with his barren
Skull across the arm-rest while the kid
Got his head between his mama's legs and slept. The poison
That replaces air took over.
And they sat—as though paralysis preceding death
Had nailed them there. The track bent south.
I saw her pulsing crotch . . . the lice rooted in that baby's hair.

THE EGG

I

Everything went in the car.
Slept in the car, slept
Like angels in the duned graveyards,
Being gone. A week's meat
Spoiled, peas
Giggled in their pods: we
Stole. And then in Edgartown
I heard my insides
Roll into a crib . . .
Washing underwear in the Atlantic
Touched the sun's sea
As light welled
That could devour water.
After Edgartown
We went the other way.

II

Until aloft beyond
The sterilizer his enormous hands
Swarmed, carnivorous,
For prey. Beneath which,
Dripping white, stripped
Open to the wand,
I saw the lamps
Converging in his glasses.
Dramamine. You let him
Rob me. But
How long? how long?
Past cutlery I saw
My body stretching like a tear
Along the paper.

III

Always nights I feel the ocean
Biting at my life. By
Inlet, in this net
Of bays, and on. Unsafe.
And on, numb
In the bourbon ripples
Of your breath
I knot . . .
Across the beach the fish
Are coming in. Without skins,
Without fins, the bare
Households of their skulls
Still fixed, piling
With the other waste.
Husks, husks. Moons
Whistle in their mouths,
Through gasping mussels.
Pried flesh. And flies
Like planets, clamped shells
Clink blindly through
Veronicas of waves . . .
The thing
Is hatching. Look. The bones
Are bending to give way.
It's dark. It's dark.
He's brought a bowl to catch
The pieces of the baby.

8

THANKSGIVING

In every room, encircled by a name-
less Southern boy from Yale,
There was my younger sister singing a Fellini theme
And making phone calls
While the rest of us kept moving her discarded boots
Or sat and drank. Outside, in twenty-
nine degrees, a stray cat
Grazed in our driveway,
Seeking waste. It scratched the pail.
There were no other sounds.
Yet on and on the preparation of that vast consoling meal
Edged toward the stove. My mother
Had the skewers in her hands.
I watched her tucking skin
As though she missed her young, while bits of onion
Misted snow over the pronged death.

HESITATE TO CALL

Lived to see you throwing
Me aside. That fought
Like netted fish inside me. Saw you throbbing
In my syrups. Saw you sleep. And lived to see
That all that all flushed down
The refuse. Done?
It lives in me.
You live in me. Malignant.
Love, you ever want me, don't.

MY COUSIN IN APRIL

Under cerulean, amid her backyard's knobby rhubarb squats
My cousin to giggle with her baby, pat
His bald top. From a window I can catch them mull basil,
Glinty silica, sienna through the ground's brocade
Of tarragon or pause under the oblong shade
Of the garage. The nervous, emerald
Fanning of some rhizome skims my cousin's knee
As up and down she bends to the baby.
I'm knitting sweaters for her second child.
As though, down miles of dinners, had not heard her rock her
    bed
In rage and thought it years she lay, locked in that tantrum . . .
Oh but such stir as in her body had to come round. Amid
    violet,
Azalea, round around the whole arriving garden
Now with her son she passes what I paused
To catch, the early bud phases, on the springing grass.

RETURNING A LOST CHILD

Nothing moves. In its cage, the broken
Blossom of a fan sways
Limply, trickling its wire, as her thin
Arms, hung like flypaper, twist about the boy . . .
Later, blocking the doorway, tongue
Pinned to the fat wedge of his pop, he watches
As I find the other room, the father strung
On crutches, waiting to be roused . . .
Now squeezed from thanks the woman's lemonade lies
In my cup. As endlessly she picks
Her spent kleenex into dust, always
Staring at that man, hearing the click,
Click of his brain's whirling empty spindle . . .

LABOR DAY

Requiring something lovely on his arm
Took me to Stamford, Connecticut, a quasi-farm,
His family's; later picking up the mammoth
Girlfriend of Charlie, meanwhile trying to pawn me off
On some third guy also up for the weekend.
But Saturday we still were paired; spent
It sprawled across that sprawling acreage
Until the grass grew limp
With damp. Like me. Johnston-baby, I can still see
The pelted clover, burrs' prickle fur and gorged
Pastures spewing infinite tiny bells. You pimp.

THE WOUND

The air stiffens to a crust.
From bed I watch
Clots of flies, crickets
Frisk and titter. Now
The weather is such grease.
All day I smell the roasts
Like presences. You
Root into your books.
You do your stuff.
In here my bedroom walls
Are paisley, like a plot
Of embryos. I lie here,
Waiting for its kick.
My love. My tenant.
As the shrubs grow
Downy, bloom and seed.
The hedges grow downy
And seed and moonlight
Burbles through the gauze.
Sticky curtains. Faking scrabble
With the pair next door
I watched you clutch your blank.
They're both on Nembutal,
The killer pill.

And I am fixed. Gone careful,
Begging for the nod,
You hover loyally above my head. I close
My eyes. And now
The prison falls in place:
Ripe things sway in the light,
Parts of plants, leaf
Fragments . . .
You are covering the cot
With sheets. I feel
No end. No end. It stalls
In me. It's still alive.

SILVERPOINT

My sister, by the chiming kinks
Of the Atlantic Ocean, takes in light.
Beyond her, wreathed in algae, links on links
Of breakers meet and disconnect, foam through bracelets
Of seabirds. The wind sinks. She does not feel the change
At once. It will take time. My sister,
Stirring briefly to arrange
Her towel, browns like a chicken, under fire.

EARLY DECEMBER IN CROTON-ON-HUDSON

Spiked sun. The Hudson's
Whittled down by ice.
I hear the bone dice
Of blown gravel clicking. Bone-
pale, the recent snow
Fastens like fur to the river.
Standstill. We were leaving to deliver
Christmas presents when the tire blew
Last year. Above the dead valves pines pared
Down by a storm stood, limbs bared . . .
I want you.

II

The Edge

THE EDGE

Time and again, time and again I tie
My heart to that headboard
While my quilted cries
Harden against his hand. He's bored—
I see it. Don't I lick his bribes, set his bouquets
In water? Over Mother's lace I watch him drive into the gored
Roasts, deal slivers in his mercy . . . I can feel his thighs
Against me for the children's sakes. Reward?
Mornings, crippled with this house,
I see him toast his toast and test
His coffee, hedgingly. The waste's my breakfast.

GRANDMOTHER IN THE GARDEN

The grass below the willow
Of my daughter's wash is curled
With earthworms, and the world
Is measured into row on row
Of unspiced houses, painted to seem real.
The drugged Long Island summer sun drains
Pattern from those empty sleeves, beyond my grandson
Squealing in his pen. I have survived my life.
The yellow daylight lines the oak leaf
And the wire vines melt with the unchanged changes
Of the baby. My children have their husbands' hands.
My husband's framed, propped bald as a baby on their pianos,
My tremendous man. I close my eyes. And all the clothes
I have thrown out come back to me, the hollows
Of my daughters' slips . . . they drift; I see the sheer
Summer cottons drift, equivalent to air.

PICTURES OF THE PEOPLE
IN THE WAR

Later I'll pull down the shade
And let this fluid draw life out of the paper.
Telling how. Except instead
Of showing you equipment I would first off share
My vision of the thing: the angle of that head
Submerged in fixer there, the bare
Soul in its set; you see, it's done with speed
And lighting but my point is that one never
Gets so close to anyone within experience. I took
These pictures of the people in the war
About a year ago—their hands were opening to me like
Language; tanks and dwellings meanwhile misty in the rear.

THE RACER'S WIDOW

The elements have merged into solicitude.
Spasms of violets rise above the mud
And weed and soon the birds and ancients
Will be starting to arrive, bereaving points
South. But never mind. It is not painful to discuss
His death. I have been primed for this,
For separation, for so long. But still his face assaults
Me, I can hear that car careen again, the crowd coagulate on
    asphalt
In my sleep. And watching him, I feel my legs like snow
That let him finally let him go
As he lies draining there. And see
How even he did not get to keep that lovely body.

PORTRAIT OF THE QUEEN IN TEARS

As my father, the late star, once told me,
Son, he told me, son, and all the while
That emerald fortune mewing on his pinky,
Satin wallowing about his shoulders
With his latest wife, fat
Misfit, so profoundly straight
She tried to own me in her Rolls
As Muriel, my mother, spread their staircase
With the surfeit of her dress
Before that party wound up in the garden.
Where—myself! myself!—O oven-
fresh and black from Mexico—they kept me
Soloing right into dawn
When the musicians quit as, far away,
The pool foamed with dim, lit chickies . . .
Past which, in that still grass
Beyond the canopies, my father's ex-
Producer drifted petals on her lifted mound
As Mama held the gauze body of some girl across
Her legs . . . I have not always lived like this,
You know. And yet my sequined, consequential past
Enables me to bear these shrieking nights
And disasters. I do not mean you. No, you, love,
Are as delightful as those coupled dancers strung
Like hand props down the back lawn
Of my former mansion,
Wherever that was, or as I was
When my mother's boys would rise and stir
Like dogs for me, make offers,
Women oozing from their stays
Go wild . . . I also was a hot property in those days.

BRIDAL PIECE

Our honeymoon
He planted us by
Water. It was March. The moon
Lurched like searchlights, like
His murmurings across my brain—
He had to have his way. As down
The beach the wet wind
Snored . . . I want
My innocence. I see
My family frozen in the doorway
Now, unchanged, unchanged. Their rice congeals
Around his car. He locked our bedroll
In the trunk for laughs, later, at the deep
End. Rockaway. He reaches for me in his sleep.

My Neighbor in the Mirror

M. le professeur in prominent senility
Across the hall tidies his collected prose
And poems. Returning from a shopping spree
Not long ago, I caught him pausing to pose
Before the landing mirror in grandiose semi-profile.
It being impossible to avoid encounter on the stairs
I thought it best to smile
Openly, as though we two held equal shares
In the indiscretion. But his performance of a nod
Was labored and the infinite *politesse* of rose palm
Unfurled for salutation fraud–
ulent. At any rate, lately there's been some
Change in his schedule. He receives without zeal
Now and, judging by his refuse, eats little but oatmeal.

Sometimes at night I think of how we did
It, me nailed in her like steel, her
Over-eager on the striped contour
Sheet (I later burned it) and it makes me glad
I told her—in the kitchen cutting homemade bread—
She always did too much—I told her Sorry baby you have had
Your share. (I found her stain had dried into my hair.)
She cried. Which still does not explain my nightmares:
How she surges like her yeast dough through the door-
way shrieking It is I, love, back in living color
After all these years.

THE LADY IN THE SINGLE

Cloistered as the snail and conch
In Edgartown where the Atlantic
Rises to deposit junk
On plush, extensive sand and the pedantic

Meet for tea, amid brouhaha
I have managed this peripheral still,
Wading just steps below
The piles of overkill:

Jellyfish. But I have seen
The slick return of one that oozed back
On a breaker. Marketable sheen.
The stuffed hotel. A shy, myopic

Sailor loved me once, near here.
The summer house we'd taken for July
Was white that year, bare
Shingle; he could barely see

To kiss, still tried to play
Croquet with the family—like a girl almost,
With loosed hair on her bouquet
Of compensating flowers. I thought I was past

The memory. And yet his ghost
Took shape in smoke above the pan roast.
Five years. In tenebris the catapulted heart drones
Like Andromeda. No one telephones.

THE CRIPPLE IN THE SUBWAY

For awhile I thought had gotten
Used to it (the leg) and hardly heard
That down-hard, down-hard
Upon wood, cement, etc. of the iron
Trappings and I'd tell myself the memories
Would also disappear, tick-
ing jump-ropes and the bike, the bike
That flew beneath my sister, froze
Light, bent back its
Stinging in a flash of red chrome brighter
Than my brace or brighter
Than the morning whirling past this pit
Flamed with rush horror and their thin
Boots flashing on and on, all that easy kidskin.

NURSE'S SONG

As though I'm fooled. That lacy body managed to forget
That I have eyes, ears; dares to spring her boyfriends on the
    child.
This afternoon she told me, "Dress the baby in his crochet
Dress," and smiled. Just that. Just smiled,
Going. She is never here. O innocence, your bathinet
Is clogged with gossip, she's a sinking ship,
Your mother. Wouldn't spoil her breasts.
I hear your deaf-numb papa fussing for his tea. Sleep, sleep,
My angel, nestled with your orange bear.
Scream when her lover pats your hair.

Seconds

Craved, having so long gone
Empty, what he had, hardness
That (my boy half-grown)
Still sucked me toward that ring, that bless-
ing. Though I knew how it is sickness
In him: lounging in gin
He knots some silken threat until
He'll twist my arm, my words—my son
Stands rigid in the doorway, seeing all,
And then that fast fist rips across my only
Child, my life . . . I care, I care.
I watch the neighbors coming at me
With their views. Now huge with cake their
White face floats above its cup; they smile,
Sunken women, sucking at their tea . . .
I'd let my house go up in flame for this fire.

LETTER FROM OUR MAN IN BLOSSOMTIME

Often an easterly churns
Emerald feathered ferns
Calling to mind Aunt Rae's decrepit
Framed fan as it
Must have flickered in its heyday.
Black-eyed Susans rim blueberry. Display,
However, is all on the outside. Let me describe the utter
Simplicity of our housekeeping. The water
Stutters fits and starts in both sinks, remaining
Dependably pure ice; veining
The ceiling, a convention of leaks
Makes host of our home to any and all weather. Everything
    creaks:
Floor, shutters, the door. Still,
We have the stupendously adequate scenery to keep our morale
Afloat. And even Margaret's taking mouseholes in the molding
Fairly well in stride. But O my friend, I'm holding
Back epiphany. Last night,
More acutely than for any first time, her white
Forearms, bared in ruth-
less battle with the dinner, pierced me; I saw
Venus among those clamshells, raw
Botticelli: I have known no happiness so based in truth.

THE CELL

(Jeanne des Anges, Prioress of the Ursuline nuns,
Loudun, France: 1635)

It's always there. My back's
Bulging through linen: God
Damaged me—made
Unfit to guide, I guide.
Yet are they silent at their work.
I walk
The garden in the afternoon, who hid
Delusions under my habits
For my self was empty . . . But HE did
It, yes.
        My Father,
Lying here, I hear
The sun creak past granite
Into air, still it is night inside.
I hide and pray. And dawn,
Alone all ways, I can feel the fingers
Stir on me again like bless-
ing and the bare
Hump mount, tranquil in darkness.

THE ISLANDER

Sugar I am CALLING you. Not
Journeyed all these years for this:
You stalking chicken in the subways,
Nights hunched in alleys all to get
That pinch . . . O heartbit,
Fastened to the chair.
The supper's freezing in the dark.
While I, my prince, my prince . . .
Your fruit lights up.
I watch your hands pulling at the grapes.

LETTER FROM PROVENCE

Beside the bridge's photogen-
ic lapse into air you'll
Find more interesting material.
In July the sun
Flatters your Popes' delicate
City as always, turning granite
Gold. The slum's at standstill then,
Choking with droppings. Still
Its children are not entirely hostile;
Proffer smiles
At intervals most charmingly. I gave
Them chocolate, softened in the heat,
Which they would not
Go near. We heard they live on love.

MEMO FROM THE CAVE

O love, you airtight bird,
My mouse-brown
Alibis hang upside-down
Above the pegboard
With its dangled pots
I don't have chickens for;
My lies are crawling on the floor
Like families but their larvae will not
Leave this nest. I've let
Despair bed
Down in your stead
And wet
Our quilted cover
So the rot–
scent of its pussy-foot–
ing fingers lingers, when it's over.

FIRSTBORN

The weeks go by. I shelve them,
They are all the same, like peeled soup cans . . .
Beans sour in their pot. I watch the lone onion
Floating like Ophelia, caked with grease:
You listless, fidget with the spoon.
What now? You miss my care? Your yard ripens
To a ward of roses, like a year ago when staff nuns
Wheeled me down the aisle . . .
You couldn't look. I saw
Converted love, your son,
Drooling under glass, starving . . .

We are eating well.
Today my meatman turns his trained knife
On veal, your favorite. I pay with my life.

LA FORCE

Made me what I am.
Gray, glued to her dream
Kitchen, among bones, among these
Dripping willows squatted to imbed
A bulb: I tend her plot. Her pride
And joy she said. I have no pride.
The lawn thins; overfed,
Her late roses gag on fertilizer past the tool
House. Now the cards are cut.
She cannot eat, she cannot take the stairs—
My life is sealed. The woman with the hound
Comes up but she will not be harmed.
I have the care of her.

THE GAME

And yet I've lived like this for years.
All since he quit me—caught the moon as round as aspirin
While, across the hall, the heartfelt murmurs
Of the queers . . . I see my punishment revolving in its den:

Around. Around. There should have been
A lesson somewhere. In Geneva, the ferocious local whore
Lay peeled for absolution with a tricot membrane
Sticking to her skin. I don't remember

How it happened that I saw. The place was filthy. She would sit
And pick her feet until they knocked. Like Customs. She'd just
    wait.

III

Cottonmouth Country

COTTONMOUTH COUNTRY

Fish bones walked the waves off Hatteras.
And there were other signs
That Death wooed us, by water, wooed us
By land: among the pines
An uncurled cottonmouth that rolled on moss
Reared in the polluted air.
Birth, not death, is the hard loss.
I know. I also left a skin there.

PHENOMENAL SURVIVALS OF DEATH IN NANTUCKET

I

Here in Nantucket does the tiny soul
Confront water. Yet this element is not foreign soil;
I see the water as extension of my mind,
The troubled part, and waves the waves of mind
When in Nantucket they collapsed in epilepsy
On the bare shore. I see
A shawled figure when I am asleep who says, "Our lives
Are strands between the miracles of birth
And death. I am Saint Elizabeth.
In my basket are knives."
Awake I see Nantucket, the familiar earth.

II

Awake I see Nantucket but with this bell
Of voice I can toll you token of regions below visible:
On the third night came
A hurricane; my Saint Elizabeth came
Not and nothing could prevent the rent
Craft from its determined end. Waves dent-
ed with lightning launched my loosed mast
To fly downward, I following. They do not tell
You but bones turned coral still smell
Amid forsaken treasure. I have been past
What you hear in a shell.

III

Past what you hear in a shell, the roar,
Is the true bottom: infamous calm. The doctor
Having shut the door sat me down, took ropes
Out of reach, firearms, and with high hopes
Promised that Saint Elizabeth carried
Only foodstuffs or some flowers for charity, nor was I buried
Under the vacation island of Nantucket where
Beach animals dwell in relative compatibility and peace.
Flies, snails. Asleep I saw these
Beings as complacent angels of the land and air.
When dawn comes to the sea's

IV

Acres of shining white body in Nantucket
I shall not remember otherwise but wear a locket
With my lover's hair inside
And walk like a bride, and wear him inside.
From these shallows expands
The mercy of the sea.
My first house shall be built on these sands,
My second in the sea.

EASTER SEASON

There is almost no sound . . . only the redundant stir
Of shrubs as perfumed temperatures embalm
Our coast. I saw the spreading gush of people with their palms.
In Westchester, the crocus spreads like cancer.

This will be the death of me. I feel the leaves close in,
Promise threaten from all sides and above.
It is not real. The green seed-pod, flaky dove
Of the bud descend. The rest is risen.

SCRAPS

We had codes
In our house. Like
Locks; they said
We never lock
Our door to you.
And never did.
Their bed
Stood, spotless as a tub . . .
I passed it every day
For twenty years, until
I went my way. My chore
Was marking time. Gluing
Relics into books I saw
Myself at seven learning
Distance at my mother's knee.
My favorite snapshot of my
Father shows him pushing forty
And lyrical
Above his firstborn's empty face.
The usual miracle.

THE TREE HOUSE

The pail droops on chain, rotten,
Where the well's been
Rinsed with bog, as round and round
The reed-weed rockets down Deer Island
Amid frosted spheres of acid: berry pick-
ing. All day long I watched the land break
Up into the ocean. Happened long ago,
And lost—what isn't—bits of jetty go
Their private ways, or sink, trailing water.
Little's left. Past this window where
My mother's basil drowned
In salad, I can see our orchard, balsams
Clenched around their birds. The basil flourished on
Neglect. Open my room, trees. Child's come.

MERIDIAN

Long Island Sound's
Asleep: no wind
Rustles down the inlet
In the sagging light
As, stalled at
Vanishing, two Sunday sailboats
Wait it out,
Paralysis, or peace,
Whichever, and the drained sun
Sinks through insects coalesced
To mist, mosquitoes
Rippling over the muddy ocean.

LATE SNOW

Seven years I watched the next-door
Lady stroll her empty mate. One May he turned his head to see
A chrysalis give forth its kleenex creature:

He'd forgotten what they were. But pleasant days she
Walked him up and down. And crooned to him.
He gurgled from his wheelchair, finally

Dying last Fall. I think the birds came
Back too soon this year. The slugs
Have been extinguished by a snow. Still, all the same,

She wasn't young herself. It must have hurt her legs
To push his weight that way. A late snow hugs
The robins' tree. I saw it come. The mama withers on her eggs.

To Florida

Southward floated over
The vicious little houses, down
The land. Past Carolina, where
The bloom began
Beneath their throbbing clouds, they fed us
Coldcuts, free. We had our choice.
Below, the seasons twist; years
Roll backward toward the can
Like film, and the mistake appears,
To scale, soundlessly. The signs
Light up. Across the aisle
An old man twitches in his sleep. His mind
Will firm in time. His health
Will meet him at the terminal.

THE SLAVE SHIP

Sir: Cruising for profit
Close to Portsmouth we have not
Done well. All winds
Quarrel with our course it seems and daily the crew whines
For fresh woman-
flesh or blood again. No gain
Accumulates; this time I fear with reason. There's no
Other news. A week ago
We charged a trader stocked with Africans
I knew for royal but their skin fixed terror in my men's
Eyes—against my will they mounted her and in the slow
Dawn off Georgia stole her whole
Hold's gold and slew that living cargo.

SOLSTICE

June's edge. The sun
Turns kind. Birds wallow in the sob of pure air,
Crated from the coast . . . Un-
real. Unreal. I see the cure

Dissolving on the screen. Outside, dozing
In its sty, the neighbors' offspring
Sucks its stuffed monster, given
Time. And now the end begins:

Packaged words. He purrs his need again.
The rest is empty. Stoned, stone-
blind she totters to the lock
Through webs of diapers. It is Christmas on the clock,

A year's precise,
Terrible ascent, climaxed in ice.

THE INLET

Words fail me. The ocean traveling stone
Returns turquoise; small animals twinkle in a haze
Of weed as this or that sequence
Of pod rattles with complete delicacy on the rotten vine.
I know what's slipping through my fingers.
In Hatteras the stones were oiled with mud.
The sunset leaked like steak blood,
Sank, and my companion weaved his fingers
Through my fingers. Wood's Hole,
Edgartown, the Vineyard in the rain,
The Vineyard not in the rain, the rain
Fuming like snow in Worcester, like gas in the coal
Country. Grass and goldenrod come to me,
Milkweed covers me over, and reed. But this riddle
Has no name: I saw a blind baby try
To fix its fists in tendrils
Of its mother's hair, and get air. The air burns,
The seaweed hisses in its cistern . . .

    Waveside, beside earth's edge,
    Before the toward-death cartwheel of the sun,
    I dreamed I was afraid and through the din
    Of birds, the din, the hurricane of parting sedge
    Came to the danger lull.
    The white weeds, white waves' white
    Scalps dissolve in the obliterating light.
    And only I, Shadrach, come back alive and well.

SATURNALIA

The year turns. The wolf takes back her tit
As war eats at the empire
Past this waxworks, the eternal city.
We have had our round. What
Lords rise are not of Rome: now northward some two-bit
Vercingetorix sharpens his will. A star
Is born.   Caesar
Snores on his perch above the Senate.

This is history. Ice clogs the ducts; my friend,
I wake to frost
On marble and a chill men take for omen
Here. The myth contracts. All cast
For comfort, shun their works to pray,
Preening for Judgment. Judgment fails. One year,
Twenty—we are lost. This month the feasts begin.
Token slaves suck those dripping fowl we offer
To insure prosperity.

The House on Marshland (1975)

WITH LOVE AND GRATITUDE
KAREN KENNERLY
TOM GILSON
ELLEN BRYANT VOIGHT

I

All Hallows

ALL HALLOWS

Even now this landscape is assembling.
The hills darken. The oxen
sleep in their blue yoke,
the fields having been
picked clean, the sheaves
bound evenly and piled at the roadside
among cinquefoil, as the toothed moon rises:

This is the barrenness
of harvest or pestilence.
And the wife leaning out the window
with her hand extended, as in payment,
and the seeds
distinct, gold, calling
Come here
Come here, little one

And the soul creeps out of the tree.

THE POND

Night covers the pond with its wing.
Under the ringed moon I can make out
your face swimming among minnows and the small
echoing stars. In the night air
the surface of the pond is metal.

Within, your eyes are open. They contain
a memory I recognize, as though
we had been children together. Our ponies
grazed on the hill, they were gray
with white markings. Now they graze
with the dead who wait
like children under their granite breastplates,
lucid and helpless:

The hills are far away. They rise up
blacker than childhood.
What do you think of, lying so quietly
by the water? When you look that way I want
to touch you, but do not, seeing
as in another life we were of the same blood.

GRETEL IN DARKNESS

This is the world we wanted.
All who would have seen us dead
are dead. I hear the witch's cry
break in the moonlight through a sheet
of sugar: God rewards.
Her tongue shrivels into gas. . . .

Now, far from women's arms
and memory of women, in our father's hut
we sleep, are never hungry.
Why do I not forget?
My father bars the door, bars harm
from this house, and it is years.

No one remembers. Even you, my brother,
summer afternoons you look at me as though
you meant to leave,
as though it never happened.
But I killed for you. I see armed firs,
the spires of that gleaming kiln—

Nights I turn to you to hold me
but you are not there.
Am I alone? Spies
hiss in the stillness, Hansel,
we are there still and it is real, real,
that black forest and the fire in earnest.

FOR MY MOTHER

It was better when we were
together in one body.
Thirty years. Screened
through the green glass
of your eye, moonlight
filtered into my bones
as we lay
in the big bed, in the dark,
waiting for my father.
Thirty years. He closed
your eyelids with
two kisses. And then spring
came and withdrew from me
the absolute
knowledge of the unborn,
leaving the brick stoop
where you stand, shading
your eyes, but it is
night, the moon
is stationed in the beech tree,
round and white among
the small tin markers of the stars:
Thirty years. A marsh
grows up around the house.
Schools of spores circulate
behind the shades, drift through
gauze flutterings of vegetation.

ARCHIPELAGO

The tenth year we came upon immense sunlight, a relief
of islands locked into the water. These became our course.
Eleven months we drifted, toward the twelfth
wandered into docile ocean, a harbor. We prepared for peace.
Weeks passed. And then the captain saw
the mouth closing that defined our port—we are
devoured. Other voices stir. Water
sneers against our ship, our shrunk number runs
in two packs: madness and suicide. The twelfth year
the captain calls his name, it has no meaning, and the crew
shrieks in its extremity.

THE MAGI

Toward world's end, through the bare
beginnings of winter, they are traveling again.
How many winters have we seen it happen,
watched the same sign come forward as they pass
cities sprung around this route their gold
engraved on the desert, and yet
held our peace, these
being the Wise, come to see at the accustomed hour
nothing changed: roofs, the barn
blazing in darkness, all they wish to see.

THE SHAD-BLOW TREE

—for Tom

1 THE TREE

It is all here,
luminous water, the imprinted sapling
matched, branch by branch,
to the lengthened
tree in the lens, as it was
against the green, poisoned landscape.

2 THE LATENT IMAGE

One year he focused on a tree
until, through sunlight pure as never afterward, he saw
the season, early spring, work upon those limbs
its white flower, which the eye
retains: deep in the brain
the shad–blow coins its leaf in this context,
among monuments, continuous with such frozen forms
as have become the trained vine,
root, rock, and all things perishing.

MESSENGERS

You have only to wait, they will find you.
The geese flying low over the marsh,
glittering in black water.
They find you.

And the deer—
how beautiful they are,
as though their bodies did not impede them.
Slowly they drift into the open
through bronze panels of sunlight.

Why would they stand so still
if they were not waiting?
Almost motionless, until their cages rust,
the shrubs shiver in the wind,
squat and leafless.

You have only to let it happen:
that cry—*release, release*—like the moon
wrenched out of earth and rising
full in its circle of arrows

until they come before you
like dead things, saddled with flesh,
and you above them, wounded and dominant.

THE MURDERESS

You call me sane, insane—I tell you men
were leering to themselves; she saw.
She was my daughter. She would pare
her skirt until her thighs grew
longer, till the split tongue slid into her brain.
He had her smell. Fear
will check beauty, but she had no fear. She talked
doubletalk, she lent
her heat to Hell's: Commissioner, the sun
opens to consume the Virgin on the fifteenth day.
It was like slitting fish. And then the stain
dissolved, and God presided at her body.

FLOWERING PLUM

In spring from the black branches of the flowering plum tree
the woodthrush issues its routine
message of survival. Where does such happiness come from
as the neighbors' daughter reads into that singing,
and matches? All afternoon she sits
in the partial shade of the plum tree, as the mild wind
floods her immaculate lap with blossoms, greenish white
and white, leaving no mark, unlike
the fruit that will inscribe
unraveling dark stains in heavier winds, in summer.

NATIVITY POEM

It is the evening
of the birth of god.
Singing &
with gold instruments
the angels bear down
upon the barn, their wings
neither white
wax nor marble. So
they have been recorded:
burnished,
literal in the composed air,
they raise their harps above
the beasts likewise gathering,
the lambs & all the startled
silken chickens. . . . And Joseph,
off to one side, has touched
his cheek, meaning
he is weeping—

But how small he is, withdrawn
from the hollow of his mother's life,
the raw flesh bound
in linen as the stars yield
light to delight his sense
for whom there is no ornament.

To Autumn

—for Keith Althaus

Morning quivers in the thorns; above the budded snowdrops
caked with dew like little virgins, the azalea bush
ejects its first leaves, and it is spring again.
The willow waits its turn, the coast
is coated with a faint green fuzz, anticipating
mold. Only I
do not collaborate, having
flowered earlier. I am no longer young. What
of it? Summer approaches, and the long
decaying days of autumn when I shall begin
the great poems of my middle period.

STILL LIFE

Father has his arm around Tereze.
She squints. My thumb
is in my mouth: my fifth autumn.
Near the copper beech
the spaniel dozes in the shadows.
Not one of us does not avert his eyes.

Across the lawn, in full sun, my mother
stands behind her camera.

FOR JANE MYERS

Sap rises from the sodden ditch
and glues two green ears to the dead
birch twig. Perilous beauty—
and already Jane is digging out
her colored tennis shoes,
one mauve, one yellow, like large crocuses.

And by the laundromat
the Bartletts in their tidy yard—

as though it were not
wearying, wearying

to hear in the bushes
the mild harping of the breeze,
the daffodils flocking and honking—

Look how the bluet falls apart, mud
pockets the seed.
Months, years, then the dull blade of the wind.
It is spring! We are going to die!

And now April raises up her plaque of flowers
and the heart
expands to admit its adversary.

GRATITUDE

Do not think I am not grateful for your small
kindness to me.
I like small kindnesses.
In fact I actually prefer them to the more
substantial kindness, that is always eying you,
like a large animal on a rug,
until your whole life reduces
to nothing but waking up morning after morning
cramped, and the bright sun shining on its tusks.

POEM

In the early evening, as now, a man is bending
over his writing table.
Slowly he lifts his head; a woman
appears, carrying roses.
Her face floats to the surface of the mirror,
marked with the green spokes of rose stems.

It is a form
of suffering: then always the transparent page
raised to the window until its veins emerge
as words finally filled with ink.

And I am meant to understand
what binds them together
or to the gray house held firmly in place by dusk

because I must enter their lives:
it is spring, the pear tree
filming with weak, white blossoms.

THE SCHOOL CHILDREN

The children go forward with their little satchels.
And all morning the mothers have labored
to gather the late apples, red and gold,
like words of another language.

And on the other shore
are those who wait behind great desks
to receive these offerings.

How orderly they are—the nails
on which the children hang
their overcoats of blue or yellow wool.

And the teachers shall instruct them in silence
and the mothers shall scour the orchards for a way out,
drawing to themselves the gray limbs of the fruit trees
bearing so little ammunition.

JEANNE D'ARC

It was in the fields. The trees grew still,
a light passed through the leaves speaking
of Christ's great grace: I heard.
My body hardened into armor.

                         Since the guards
gave me over to darkness I have prayed to God
and now the voices answer I must be
transformed to fire, for God's purpose,
and have bid me kneel
to bless my King, and thank
the enemy to whom I owe my life.

Departure

My father is standing on a railroad platform.
Tears pool in his eyes, as though the face
glimmering in the window were the face of someone
he was once. But the other has forgotten;
as my father watches, he turns away,
drawing the shade over his face,
goes back to his reading.

And already in its deep groove
the train is waiting with its breath of ashes.

GEMINI

There is a soul in me
It is asking
to be given its body

It is asking
to be given blue eyes
a skull matted

with black hair
that shape
already formed & detaching

So the past put forth
a house filled with
asters & white lilac

a child
in her cotton dress
the lawn, the copper beech—

such of my own lives
I have cast off—the sunlight
chipping at the curtains

& the wicker chairs
uncovered, winter after winter,
as the stars finally

thicken & descend as snow

II

The Apple Trees

THE UNDERTAKING

The darkness lifts, imagine, in your lifetime.
There you are—cased in clean bark you drift
through weaving rushes, fields flooded with cotton.
You are free. The river films with lilies,
shrubs appear, shoots thicken into palm. And now
all fear gives way: the light
looks after you, you feel the waves' goodwill
as arms widen over the water; Love,

the key is turned. Extend yourself—
it is the Nile, the sun is shining,
everywhere you turn is luck.

POMEGRANATE

First he gave me
his heart. It was
red fruit containing
many seeds, the skin
leathery, unlikely.
I preferred
to starve, bearing
out my training.
Then he said Behold
how the world looks, minding
your mother. I
peered under his arm:
What had she done
with color & odor?
Whereupon he said Now *there*
is a woman who loves
with a vengeance, adding
Consider she is in her element:
the trees turning to her, whole
villages going under
although in hell
the bushes are still
burning with pomegranates.
At which
he cut one open & began
to suck. When he looked up at last
it was to say My dear

you are your own
woman, finally, but examine
this grief your mother
parades over our heads
remembering
that she is one to whom
these depths were not offered.

BRENNENDE LIEBE

—*1904*

Dearest love: The roses are in bloom again,
cream and rose, to either side of the brick walk.
I pass among them with my white umbrella
as the sun beats down upon the oval plots like pools
in the grass, willows and the grove
of statuary. So the days go by. Fine days
I take my tea beneath the elm
half turned, as though you were beside me saying
Flowers that could take your breath away . . .
And always on the tray
a rose, and always the sun branded on the river
and the men in summer suits, in linen, and the girls,
their skirts circled in shadow. . . . Last night
I dreamed that you did not return.
Today is fair. The little maid filled a silver bowl
shaped like a swan with roses for my bedside,
with the dark red they call *Brennende Liebe*,
which I find so beautiful.

ABISHAG

I

At God's word David's kinsmen cast
through Canaan:
It was understood
the king was dying
as they said
outright
so that my father turned to me saying
How much have I ever asked of you
to which I answered
Nothing
as I remembered

So the sun rose from his shoulders:
blue air, the desert, the small
yellowing village

When I see myself
it is still as I was then,
beside the well, staring
into the hollowed gourd half filled
with water, where the dark braid
grazing the left shoulder was recorded
though the face
was featureless
of which they did not say
She has the look of one who seeks
some greater and destroying passion:

They took me as I was.
Not one among the kinsmen touched me,
not one among the slaves.
No one will touch me now.

2

In the recurring dream my father
stands at the doorway in his black cassock
telling me to choose
among my suitors, each of whom
will speak my name once
until I lift my hand in signal.
On my father's arm I listen
for not three sounds: *Abishag,*
but two: *my love*—

I tell you if it is my own will
binding me I cannot be saved.
And yet in the dream, in the half-light
of the stone house, they looked
so much alike. Sometimes I think
the voices were themselves
identical, and that I raised my hand
chiefly in weariness. I hear my father saying
Choose, choose. But they were not alike
and to select death, O yes I can
believe that of my body.

12.6.71

You having turned from me
I dreamed we were
beside a pond between two mountains
It was night
The moon throbbed in its socket
Where the spruces thinned
three deer wakened & broke cover
and I heard my name
not spoken but cried out
so that I reached for you
except the sheet was ice
as they had come for me
who, one by one, were likewise
introduced to darkness
And the snow
which has not ceased since
began

LOVE POEM

There is always something to be made of pain.
Your mother knits.
She turns out scarves in every shade of red.
They were for Christmas, and they kept you warm
while she married over and over, taking you
along. How could it work,
when all those years she stored her widowed heart
as though the dead come back.
No wonder you are the way you are,
afraid of blood, your women
like one brick wall after another.

NORTHWOOD PATH

For my part
we are as we were
on the path
that afternoon:
it is
October, I can see
the sun sink
drawing out
our parallel
shadows. And you,
for example what
were you thinking, so
attentive to your
shoes? I recall
we spoke of
your car
the whole length
of the woods:
in so much withering
the pokeweed had
branched into its
purplish berry—so
desire called
love into being.
But always the choice
was on both sides
characteristic,
as you said,
in the dark you came
to need,
you would do it again

THE FIRE

Had you died when we were together
I would have wanted nothing of you.
Now I think of you as dead, it is better.

Often, in the cool early evenings of the spring
when, with the first leaves,
all that is deadly enters the world,
I build a fire for us of pine and apple wood;
repeatedly
the flames flare and diminish
as the night comes on in which
we see one another so clearly—

And in the days we are contented
as formerly
in the long grass,
in the woods' green doors and shadows.

And you never say
Leave me
since the dead do not like being alone.

THE FORTRESS

There is nothing now. To learn
the lesson past disease
was easier. In God's hotel I saw
my name and number stapled to a vein
as Marcy funneled its corrective air
toward Placid. I can breathe
again. I watch the mountain under siege
by ice give way to blocks of dungeons,
ovens manned by wives. I understand.
They coil their hair, they turn their
music on as, humming to herself, the night-
nurse smoothes her uniform. This is
the proper pain. The lights are out. Love
forms in the human body.

HERE ARE MY BLACK CLOTHES

I think now it is better to love no one
than to love you. Here are my black clothes,
the tired nightgowns and robes fraying
in many places. Why should they hang useless
as though I were going naked? You liked me well enough
in black; I make you a gift of these objects.
You will want to touch them with your mouth, run
your fingers through the thin
tender underthings and I
will not need them in my new life.

UNDER TAURUS

We were on the pier, you desiring
that I see the Pleiades. I could see
everything but what you wished.

Now I will follow. There is not a single cloud; the stars
appear, even the invisible sister. Show me where to look,
as though they will stay where they are.

Instruct me in the dark.

THE SWIMMER

You sat in the tub.
No sand stirred, the dead
waited in the ocean.
Then the tapwater
flooded over you,
sapphire and emerald.

The beach
is as you found it,
littered with objects.
They have brought me here;
I rifle through them,
shell and bone, and am not satisfied.

What brought me to rest was your body.
Far away you turn your head:
through still grass the wind
moves into a human language

and the darkness comes,
the long nights
pass into stationary darkness.

Only the sea moves.
It takes on color, onyx and manganese.
If you are there it will release you
as when, among the tame waves,
I saw your worn face,
your long arms making for shore—

The waves come forward,
we are traveling together.

96

THE LETTERS

It is night for the last time.
For the last time your hands
gather on my body.

Tomorrow it will be autumn.
We will sit together on the balcony
watching the dry leaves drift over the village
like the letters we will burn,
one by one, in our separate houses.

Such a quiet night.
Only your voice murmuring
You're wet, you want to
and the child
sleeps as though he were not born.

In the morning it will be autumn.
We will walk together in the small garden
among stone benches and the shrubs
still sheeted in mist
like furniture left for a long time.

Look how the leaves drift in the darkness.
We have burned away
all that was written on them.

JAPONICA

The trees are flowering
on the hill.
They are bearing
large solitary blossoms,
japonica,
as when you came to me
mistakenly
carrying such flowers
having snapped them
from the thin branches.
The rain had stopped. Sunlight
motioned through the leaves.
But death
also has its flower,
it is called
contagion, it is
red or white, the color
of japonica—
You stood there,
your hands full of flowers.
How could I not take them
since they were a gift?

THE APPLE TREES

Your son presses against me
his small intelligent body.

I stand beside his crib
as in another dream
you stood among trees hung
with bitten apples
holding out your arms.
I did not move
but saw the air dividing
into panes of color—at the very last
I raised him to the window saying
See what you have made
and counted out the whittled ribs,
the heart on its blue stalk
as from among the trees
the darkness issued:

In the dark room your son sleeps.
The walls are green, the walls
are spruce and silence.
I wait to see how he will leave me.
Already on his hand the map appears
as though you carved it there,
the dead fields, women rooted to the river.

Descending Figure
(1980)

I

The Garden

THE DROWNED CHILDREN

You see, they have no judgment.
So it is natural that they should drown,
first the ice taking them in
and then, all winter, their wool scarves
floating behind them as they sink
until at last they are quiet.
And the pond lifts them in its manifold dark arms.

But death must come to them differently,
so close to the beginning.
As though they had always been
blind and weightless. Therefore
the rest is dreamed, the lamp,
the good white cloth that covered the table,
their bodies.

And yet they hear the names they used
like lures slipping over the pond:
What are you waiting for
come home, come home, lost
in the waters, blue and permanent.

THE GARDEN

1 THE FEAR OF BIRTH

One sound. Then the hiss and whir
of houses gliding into their places.
And the wind
leafs through the bodies of animals—

But my body that could not content itself
with health—why should it be sprung back
into the chord of sunlight?

It will be the same again.
This fear, this inwardness,
until I am forced into a field
without immunity
even to the least shrub that walks
stiffly out of the dirt, trailing
the twisted signature of its root,
even to a tulip, a red claw.

And then the losses,
one after another,
all supportable.

2 THE GARDEN

The garden admires you.
For your sake it smears itself with green pigment,
the ecstatic reds of the roses,
so that you will come to it with your lovers.

And the willows—
see how it has shaped these green
tents of silence. Yet
there is still something you need,
your body so soft, so alive, among the stone animals.

Admit that it is terrible to be like them,
beyond harm.

3 THE FEAR OF LOVE

That body lying beside me like obedient stone—
once its eyes seemed to be opening,
we could have spoken.

At that time it was winter already.
By day the sun rose in its helmet of fire
and at night also, mirrored in the moon.
Its light passed over us freely,
as though we had lain down
in order to leave no shadows,
only these two shallow dents in the snow.
And the past, as always, stretched before us,
still, complex, impenetrable.

How long did we lie there
as, arm in arm in their cloaks of feathers,
the gods walked down
from the mountain we built for them?

4 ORIGINS

As though a voice were saying
You should be asleep by now—
But there was no one. Nor
had the air darkened,
though the moon was there,
already filled in with marble.

As though, in a garden crowded with flowers,
a voice had said
How dull they are, these golds,
so sonorous, so repetitious
until you closed your eyes,
lying among them, all
stammering flame:

And yet you could not sleep,
poor body, the earth
still clinging to you—

5 THE FEAR OF BURIAL

In the empty field, in the morning,
the body waits to be claimed.
The spirit sits beside it, on a small rock—
nothing comes to give it form again.

Think of the body's loneliness.
At night pacing the sheared field,
its shadow buckled tightly around.
Such a long journey.

And already the remote, trembling lights of the village
not pausing for it as they scan the rows.
How far away they seem,
the wooden doors, the bread and milk
laid like weights on the table.

PALAIS DES ARTS

Love long dormant showing itself:
the large expected gods
caged really, the columns
sitting on the lawn, as though perfection
were not timeless but stationary—that
is the comedy, she thinks,
that they are paralyzed. Or like the matching swans,
insular, circling the pond: restraint so passionate
implies possession. They hardly speak.
On the other bank, a small boy throws bits of bread
into the water. The reflected monument
is stirred, briefly, stricken with light—
She can't touch his arm in innocence again.
They have to give that up and begin
as male and female, thrust and ache.

PIETÀ

Under the strained
fabric of her skin, his heart
stirred. She listened,
because he had no father.
So she knew
he wanted to stay
in her body, apart
from the world
with its cries, its
roughhousing,
but already the men
gather to see him
born: they crowd in
or kneel at worshipful
distance, like
figures in a painting
whom the star lights, shining
steadily in its dark context.

DESCENDING FIGURE

1 THE WANDERER

At twilight I went into the street.
The sun hung low in the iron sky,
ringed with cold plumage.
If I could write to you
about this emptiness—
Along the curb, groups of children
were playing in the dry leaves.
Long ago, at this hour, my mother stood
at the lawn's edge, holding my little sister.
Everyone was gone; I was playing
in the dark street with my other sister,
whom death had made so lonely.
Night after night we watched the screened porch
filling with a gold, magnetic light.
Why was she never called?
Often I would let my own name glide past me
though I craved its protection.

2 THE SICK CHILD

—Rijksmuseum

A small child
is ill, has wakened.
It is winter, past midnight
in Antwerp. Above a wooden chest,
the stars shine.
And the child
relaxes in her mother's arms.
The mother does not sleep;
she stares
fixedly into the bright museum.
By spring the child will die.
Then it is wrong, wrong
to hold her—
Let her be alone,
without memory, as the others wake
terrified, scraping the dark
paint from their faces.

3 FOR MY SISTER

Far away my sister is moving in her crib.
The dead ones are like that,
always the last to quiet.

Because, however long they lie in the earth,
they will not learn to speak
but remain uncertainly pressing against the wooden bars,
so small the leaves hold them down.

Now, if she had a voice,
the cries of hunger would be beginning.
I should go to her;
perhaps if I sang very softly,
her skin so white,
her head covered with black feathers. . . .

THANKSGIVING

They have come again to graze the orchard,
knowing they will be denied.
The leaves have fallen; on the dry ground
the wind makes piles of them, sorting
all its destroys.

What doesn't move, the snow will cover.
It will give them away; their hooves
make patterns which the snow remembers.
In the cleared field, they linger
as the summoned prey whose part
is not to forgive. They can afford to die.
They have their place in the dying order.

II

The Mirror

EPITHALAMIUM

There were others; their bodies
were a preparation.
I have come to see it as that.

As a stream of cries.
So much pain in the world—the formless
grief of the body, whose language
is hunger—

And in the hall, the boxed roses:
what they mean

is chaos. Then begins
the terrible charity of marriage,
husband and wife
climbing the green hill in gold light
until there is no hill,
only a flat plain stopped by the sky.

Here is my hand, he said.
But that was long ago.
Here is my hand that will not harm you.

ILLUMINATIONS

1

My son squats in the snow in his blue snowsuit.
All around him stubble, the brown
degraded bushes. In the morning air
they seem to stiffen into words.
And, between, the white steady silence.
A wren hops on the airstrip
under the sill, drills
for sustenance, then spreads
its short wings, shadows
dropping from them.

2

Last winter he could barely speak.
I moved his crib to face the window:
in the dark mornings
he would stand and grip the bars
until the walls appeared,
calling *light, light,*
that one syllable, in
demand or recognition.

3

He sits at the kitchen window
with his cup of apple juice.
Each tree forms where he left it,
leafless, trapped in his breath.
How clear their edges are,
no limb obscured by motion,
as the sun rises
cold and single over the map of language.

THE MIRROR

Watching you in the mirror I wonder
what it is like to be so beautiful
and why you do not love
but cut yourself, shaving
like a blind man. I think you let me stare
so you can turn against yourself
with greater violence,
needing to show me how you scrape the flesh away
scornfully and without hesitation
until I see you correctly,
as a man bleeding, not
the reflection I desire.

PORTRAIT

A child draws the outline of a body.
She draws what she can, but it is white all through,
she cannot fill in what she knows is there.
Within the unsupported line, she knows
that life is missing; she has cut
one background from another. Like a child,
she turns to her mother.

And you draw the heart
against the emptiness she has created.

TANGO

On evenings like this
twenty years ago:

We sit under the table,
the adults' hands
drum on our heads. Outside,
the street,
the contagious vernacular.

        Remember
how we used to dance? Inseparable,
back and forth across the living room,
Adios Muchachos, like an insect
moving on a mirror: envy
is a dance, too; the need to hurt
binds you to your partner.

        2

You thrashed in the crib,
your small mouth circling
the ancient repetitions.
I watched you through the bars,
both of us
actively starving. In the other room
our parents merged into the one
totemic creature:
Come, she said. *Come to Mother.*
You stood. You tottered toward
the inescapable body.

3

A dark board covers the sun.
Then the fathers come,
their long cars move slowly down the street,
parting the children. Then
the street is given over to darkness.

The rest follows: the labored
green of the yards, the little gardens
darned with green thread—

The trees also, whose shadows
were blue spokes.

But some the light chooses.
How they tremble
as the moon mounts them, brutal and sisterly:

I used to watch them,
all night absorbed in the moon's neutral silver
until they were finally blurred, disfigured. . . .

4

What was it like to be led?

I trusted no one. My name
was like a stranger's,
read from an envelope.

But nothing was taken from me
that I could have used.
For once, I admit that.

In the hall, posed
for the record's
passionate onset, ages
five and seven:

You were the gold sun on the horizon.
I was the judgment, my shadow
preceded me, not wavering

but like a mold that would be used again.
Your bare feet
became a woman's feet, always
saying two things at once.

Of two sisters
one is always the watcher,
one the dancer.

SWANS

You were both quiet, looking out over the water.
It was not now; it was years ago,
before you were married.
The sky above the sea had turned
the odd pale peach color of early evening
from which the sea withdrew, bearing
its carved boats: your bodies were like that.
But her face was raised to you,
against the dull waves, simplified
by passion. Then you raised your hand
and from beyond the frame of the dream
swans came to settle on the scaled water.
The sea lay mild as a pool. At its edge,
you faced her, saying
These are yours to keep. The horizon burned,
releasing its withheld light.
And then I woke. But for days
when I tried to imagine you leaving your wife
I saw her motionless before your gift:
always the swans glide unmenacing across
the rigid blue of the Pacific Ocean, then rise
in a single wave, pure white and devouring.

NIGHT PIECE

He knows he will be hurt.
The warnings come to him in bed
because repose threatens him: in the camouflaging
light of the nightlight, he pretends to guard
the flesh in which his life is summarized.
He spreads his arms. On the wall, a corresponding figure
links him to the darkness he cannot control.
In its forms, the beasts originate
who are his enemies. He cannot sleep
apart from them.

PORTLAND, 1968

You stand as rocks stand
to which the sea reaches
in transparent waves of longing;
they are marred, finally;
everything fixed is marred.
And the sea triumphs,
like all that is false,
all that is fluent and womanly.
From behind, a lens
opens for your body. Why
should you turn? It doesn't matter
who the witness is,
for whom you are suffering,
for whom you are standing still.

PORCELAIN BOWL

It rules out use:
in a lawn chair, the analogous
body of a woman is arranged,
and in this light
I cannot see what time has done to her.
A few leaves fall. A wind parts the long grass,
making a path going nowhere. And the hand
involuntarily lifts; it moves across her face
so utterly lost—
    The grass sways,
as though that motion were
an aspect of repose.
     Pearl white
on green. Ceramic
hand in the grass.

DEDICATION TO HUNGER

1 FROM THE SUBURBS

They cross the yard
and at the back door
the mother sees with pleasure
how alike they are, father and daughter—
I know something of that time.
The little girl purposefully
swinging her arms, laughing
her stark laugh:

It should be kept secret, that sound.
It means she's realized
that he never touches her.
She is a child; he could touch her
if he wanted to.

2 GRANDMOTHER

"Often I would stand at the window—
your grandfather
was a young man then—
waiting, in the early evening."

That is what marriage is.
I watch the tiny figure
changing to a man
as he moves toward her,
the last light rings in his hair.
I do not question
their happiness. And he rushes in
with his young man's hunger,
so proud to have taught her that:
his kiss would have been
clearly tender—

Of course, of course. Except
it might as well have been
his hand over her mouth.

3 EROS

To be male, always
to go to women
and be taken back
into the pierced flesh:

        I suppose
memory is stirred.
And the girl child
who wills herself
into her father's arms
likewise loved him
second. Nor is she told
what need to express.
There is a look one sees,
the mouth somehow desperate—

Because the bond
cannot be proven.

4 THE DEVIATION

It begins quietly
in certain female children:
the fear of death, taking as its form
dedication to hunger,
because a woman's body
is a grave; it will accept
anything. I remember
lying in bed at night
touching the soft, digressive breasts,
touching, at fifteen,
the interfering flesh
that I would sacrifice
until the limbs were free
of blossom and subterfuge: I felt
what I feel now, aligning these words—
it is the same need to perfect,
of which death is the mere byproduct.

5 SACRED OBJECTS

Today in the field I saw
the hard, active buds of the dogwood
and wanted, as we say, to capture them,
to make them eternal. That is the premise
of renunciation: the child,
having no self to speak of,
comes to life in denial—

I stood apart in that achievement,
in that power to expose
the underlying body, like a god
for whose deed
there is no parallel in the natural world.

HAPPINESS

A man and woman lie on a white bed.
It is morning. I think
Soon they will waken.
On the bedside table is a vase
of lilies; sunlight
pools in their throats.
I watch him turn to her
as though to speak her name
but silently, deep in her mouth—
At the window ledge,
once, twice,
a bird calls.
And then she stirs; her body
fills with his breath.

I open my eyes; you are watching me.
Almost over this room
the sun is gliding.
Look at your face, you say,
holding your own close to me
to make a mirror.
How calm you are. And the burning wheel
passes gently over us.

III

Lamentations

AUTUMNAL

Public sorrow, the acquired
gold of the leaf, the falling off,
the prefigured burning of the yield:
which is accomplished. At the lake's edge,
the metal pails are full vats of fire.
So waste is elevated
into beauty. And the scattered dead
unite in one consuming vision of order.
In the end, everything is bare.
Above the cold, receptive earth
the trees bend. Beyond,
the lake shines, placid, giving back
the established blue of heaven.
          The word
is *bear*: you give and give, you empty yourself
into a child. And you survive
the automatic loss. Against inhuman landscape,
the tree remains a figure for grief; its form
is forced accommodation. At the grave,
it is the woman, isn't it, who bends,
the spear useless beside her.

AUBADE

Today above the gull's call
I heard you waking me again
to see that bird, flying
so strangely over the city,
not wanting
to stop, wanting
the blue waste of the sea—

Now it skirts the suburb,
the noon light violent against it:

I feel its hunger
as your hand inside me,

a cry
so common, unmusical—

Ours were not
different. They rose
from the unexhausted
need of the body

fixing a wish to return:
the ashen dawn, our clothes
not sorted for departure.

APHRODITE

A woman exposed as rock
has this advantage:
she controls the harbor.
Ultimately, men appear,
weary of the open.
So terminates, they feel,
a story. In the beginning,
longing. At the end, joy.
In the middle, tedium.

In time, the young wife
naturally hardens. Drifting
from her side, in imagination,
the man returns not to a drudge
but to the goddess he projects.

On a hill, the armless figure
welcomes the delinquent boat,
her thighs cemented shut, barring
the fault in the rock.

ROSY

When you walked in with your suitcase, leaving
the door open so the night showed
in a black square behind you, with its little stars
like nailheads, I wanted to tell you
you were like the dog that came to you by default,
on three legs: now that she is again no one's,
she pursues her more durable relationships
with traffic and cold nature, as though at pains
to wound herself so that she will not heal.
She is past being taken in by kindness,
preferring wet streets: what death claims
it does not abandon.
You understand, the animal means nothing to me.

The Dream of Mourning

I sleep so you will be alive,
it is that simple.
The dreams themselves are nothing.
They are the sickness you control,
nothing more.

I rush toward you in the summer twilight,
not in the real world, but in the buried one
where you are waiting,
as the wind moves over the bay, toying with it,
forcing thin ridges of panic—

And then the morning comes, demanding prey.
Remember? And the world complies.

Last night was different.
Someone fucked me awake; when I opened my eyes
it was over, all the need gone
by which I knew my life.
And for one instant I believed I was entering
the stable dark of the earth
and thought it would hold me.

THE GIFT

Lord, You may not recognize me
speaking for someone else.
I have a son. He is
so little, so ignorant.
He likes to stand
at the screen door, calling
oggie, oggie, entering
language, and sometimes
a dog will stop and come up
the walk, perhaps
accidentally. May he believe
this is not an accident?
At the screen
welcoming each beast
in love's name, Your emissary.

WORLD BREAKING APART

I look out over the sterile snow.
Under the white birch tree, a wheelbarrow.
The fence behind it mended. On the picnic table,
mounded snow, like the inverted contents of a bowl
whose dome the wind shapes. The wind,
with its impulse to build. And under my fingers,
the square white keys, each stamped
with its single character. I believed
a mind's shattering released
the objects of its scrutiny: trees, blue plums in a bowl,
a man reaching for his wife's hand
across a slatted table, and quietly covering it,
as though his will enclosed it in that gesture.
I saw them come apart, the glazed clay
begin dividing endlessly, dispersing
incoherent particles that went on
shining forever. I dreamed of watching that
the way we watched the stars on summer evenings,
my hand on your chest, the wine
holding the chill of the river. There is no such light.
And pain, the free hand, changes almost nothing.
Like the winter wind, it leaves
settled forms in the snow. Known, identifiable—
except there are no uses for them.

THE RETURN

At first when you went away
I was frightened; then
a boy touched me on the street,
his eyes were level with mine,
clear and grieving: I
called him in; I spoke to him
in our language,
but his hands were yours,
so gently making their murderous claim—
And then it didn't matter
which one of you I called,
the wound was that deep.

LAMENTATIONS

1 THE LOGOS

They were both still,
the woman mournful, the man
branching into her body.

But god was watching.
They felt his gold eye
projecting flowers on the landscape.

Who knew what he wanted?
He was god, and a monster.
So they waited. And the world
filled with his radiance,
as though he wanted to be understood.

Far away, in the void that he had shaped,
he turned to his angels.

2 NOCTURNE

A forest rose from the earth.
O pitiful, so needing
God's furious love—

Together they were beasts.
They lay in the fixed
dusk of his negligence;
from the hills, wolves came, mechanically
drawn to their human warmth,
their panic.

Then the angels saw
how He divided them:
the man, the woman, and the woman's body.

Above the churned reeds, the leaves let go
a slow moan of silver.

3 THE COVENANT

Out of fear, they built a dwelling place.
But a child grew between them
as they slept, as they tried
to feed themselves.

They set it on a pile of leaves,
the small discarded body
wrapped in the clean skin
of an animal. Against the black sky
they saw the massive argument of light.

Sometimes it woke. As it reached its hands
they understood they were the mother and father,
there was no authority above them.

4 THE CLEARING

Gradually, over many years,
the fur disappeared from their bodies
until they stood in the bright light
strange to one another.
Nothing was as before.
Their hands trembled, seeking
the familiar.

Nor could they keep their eyes
from the white flesh
on which wounds would show clearly
like words on a page.

And from the meaningless browns and greens
at last God arose, His great shadow
darkening the sleeping bodies of His children,
and leapt into heaven.

How beautiful it must have been,
the earth, that first time
seen from the air.

The Triumph of
Achilles
(1985)

I

MOCK ORANGE

It is not the moon, I tell you.
It is these flowers
lighting the yard.

I hate them.
I hate them as I hate sex,
the man's mouth
sealing my mouth, the man's
paralyzing body—

and the cry that always escapes,
the low, humiliating
premise of union—

In my mind tonight
I hear the question and pursuing answer
fused in one sound
that mounts and mounts and then
is split into the old selves,
the tired antagonisms. Do you see?
We were made fools of.
And the scent of mock orange
drifts through the window.

How can I rest?
How can I be content
when there is still
that odor in the world?

METAMORPHOSIS

1 NIGHT

The angel of death flies
low over my father's bed.
Only my mother sees. She and my father
are alone in the room.

She bends over him to touch
his hand, his forehead. She is
so used to mothering
that now she strokes his body
as she would the other children's,
first gently, then
inured to suffering.

Nothing is any different.
Even the spot on the lung
was always there.

2 METAMORPHOSIS

My father has forgotten me
in the excitement of dying.
Like a child who will not eat,
he takes no notice of anything.

I sit at the edge of his bed
while the living circle us
like so many tree stumps.

Once, for the smallest
fraction of an instant, I thought
he was alive in the present again;
then he looked at me
as a blind man stares
straight into the sun, since
whatever it could do to him
is done already.

Then his flushed face
turned away from the contract.

3 FOR MY FATHER

I'm going to live without you
as I learned once
to live without my mother.
You think I don't remember that?
I've spent my whole life trying to remember.

Now, after so much solitude,
death doesn't frighten me,
not yours, not mine either.
And those words, *the last time*,
have no power over me. I know
intense love always leads to mourning.

For once, your body doesn't frighten me.
From time to time, I run my hand over your face
lightly, like a dustcloth.
What can shock me now? I feel
no coldness that can't be explained.
Against your cheek, my hand is warm
and full of tenderness.

BROODING LIKENESS

I was born in the month of the bull,
the month of heaviness,
or of the lowered, the destructive head,
or of purposeful blindness. So I know, beyond the shadowed
patch of grass, the stubborn one, the one who doesn't look up,
still senses the rejected world. It is
a stadium, a well of dust. And you who watch him
looking down in the face of death, what do you know
of commitment? If the bull lives
one controlled act of revenge, be satisfied
that in the sky, like you, he is always moving,
not of his own accord but through the black field
like grit caught on a wheel, like shining freight.

EXILE

He did not pretend
to be one of them. They did not require
a poet, a spokesman. He saw
the dog's heart, the working
lips of the parasite—
He himself preferred
to listen in the small apartments
as a man would check his camera at the museum,
to express his commitment through silence:
there is no other exile.
The rest is egotism; in the bloody street,
the I, the impostor—
He *was* there, obsessed with revolution,
in his own city,
daily climbing the wooden stairs
that were not a path
but necessary repetitions
and for twenty years
making no poetry
of what he saw: nor did he forfeit
great achievement. In his mind,
there could be no outcry that did not equate
his choice with their imprisonment
and he would not allow
the gift to be tainted.

WINTER MORNING

1

Today, when I woke up, I asked myself
why did Christ die? Who knows
the meaning of such questions?

It was a winter morning, unbelievably cold.
So the thoughts went on,
from each question came
another question, like a twig from a branch,
like a branch from a black trunk.

2

At a time like this
a young woman traveled through the desert settlements
looking neither forward nor backward,
sitting in perfect composure on the tired animal
as the child stirred, still sealed in its profound attachment—
The husband walked slightly ahead, older, out of place;
increasingly, the mule stumbled, the path becoming
difficult in darkness, though they persisted
in a world like our world, not ruled
by man but by a statue in heaven—

3

Above the crowds representing
humankind, the lost
citizens of a remote time,

the insulted body
raised on a cross like a criminal
to die publicly

above Jerusalem, the shimmering city
while in great flocks
birds circled the body, not partial
to this form over the others

since men were all alike,
defeated by the air,

whereas in air
the body of a bird becomes a banner:

But the lesson that was needed
was another lesson.

4

In untrustworthy springtime
he was seen moving
among us like one of us

in green Judea, covered with the veil of life,
among the olive trees, among the many shapes
blurred by spring,

stopping to eat and rest, in obvious need,
among the thousand flowers,
some planted, some distributed by wind,

like all men, seeking
recognition on earth,
so that he spoke to the disciples

in a man's voice, lifting his intact hand:
was it the wind that spoke?
Or stroked Mary's hair, until she raised her eyes

no longer wounded
by his coldness, by his needless destruction
of the flesh which was her fulfillment—

This was not the sun.
This was Christ in his cocoon of light:

so they swore. And there were other witnesses
though they were all blind,
they were all swayed by love—

5

Winters are long here.
The road a dark gray, the maples gray, silvered with lichen,
and the sun low on the horizon,
white on blue; at sunset, vivid orange-red.

When I shut my eyes, it vanishes.
When I open my eyes, it reappears.
Outside, spring rain, a pulse, a film on the window.

And suddenly it is summer, all puzzling fruit and light.

SEATED FIGURE

It was as though you were a man in a wheelchair,
your legs cut off at the knee.
But I wanted you to walk.
I wanted us to walk like lovers,
arm in arm in the summer evening,
and believed so powerfully in that projection
that I had to speak, I had to press you to stand.
Why did you let me speak?
I took your silence as I took the anguish in your face,
as part of the effort to move—
It seemed I stood forever, holding out my hand.
And all that time, you could no more heal yourself
than I could accept what I saw.

MYTHIC FRAGMENT

When the stern god
approached me with his gift
my fear enchanted him
so that he ran more quickly
through the wet grass, as he insisted,
to praise me. I saw captivity
in praise; against the lyre,
I begged my father in the sea
to save me. When
the god arrived, I was nowhere,
I was in a tree forever. Reader,
pity Apollo: at the water's edge,
I turned from him, I summoned
my invisible father—as
I stiffened in the god's arms,
of his encompassing love
my father made
no other sign from the water.

HYACINTH

1

Is that an attitude for a flower, to stand
like a club at the walk; poor slain boy,
is that a way to show
gratitude to the gods? White
with colored hearts, the tall flowers
sway around you, all the other boys,
in the cold spring, as the violets open.

2

There were no flowers in antiquity
but boys' bodies, pale, perfectly imagined.
So the gods sank to human shape with longing.
In the field, in the willow grove,
Apollo sent the courtiers away.

3

And from the blood of the wound
a flower sprang, lilylike, more brilliant
than the purples of Tyre.
Then the god wept: his vital grief
flooded the earth.

4

Beauty dies: that is the source
of creation. Outside the ring of trees
the courtiers could hear
the dove's call transmit
its uniform, its inborn sorrow—
They stood listening, among the rustling willows.

Was this the god's lament?
They listened carefully. And for a short time
all sound was sad.

5

There is no other immortality:
in the cold spring, the purple violets open.
And yet, the heart is black,
there is its violence frankly exposed.
Or is it not the heart at the center
but some other word?
And now someone is bending over them,
meaning to gather them—

6

They could not wait
in exile forever.
Through the glittering grove
the courtiers ran
calling the name
of their companion
over the birds' noise,
over the willows' aimless sadness.
Well into the night they wept,
their clear tears
altering no earthly color.

The Triumph of Achilles

In the story of Patroclus
no one survives, not even Achilles
who was nearly a god.
Patroclus resembled him; they wore
the same armor.

Always in these friendships
one serves the other, one is less than the other:
the hierarchy
is always apparent, though the legends
cannot be trusted—
their source is the survivor,
the one who has been abandoned.

What were the Greek ships on fire
compared to this loss?

In his tent, Achilles
grieved with his whole being
and the gods saw

he was a man already dead, a victim
of the part that loved,
the part that was mortal.

BASKETS

1

It is a good thing,
in the marketplace
the old woman trying to decide
among the lettuces,
impartial, weighing the heads,
examining
the outer leaves, even
sniffing them to catch
a scent of earth
of which, on one head,
some trace remains—not
the substance but
the residue—so
she prefers it to
the other, more
estranged heads, it
being freshest: nodding
briskly at the vendor's wife,
she makes this preference known,
an old woman, yet
vigorous in judgment.

2

The circle of the world—
in its midst, a dog
sits at the edge of the fountain.
The children playing there,
coming and going from the village,
pause to greet him, the impulsive

losing interest in play,
in the little village of sticks
adorned with blue fragments of pottery;
they squat beside the dog
who stretches in the hot dust:
arrows of sunlight
dance around him.
Now, in the field beyond,
some great event is ending.
In twos and threes, boldly
swinging their shirts,
the athletes stroll away, scattering
red and blue, blue and dazzling purple
over the plain ground,
over the trivial surface.

3

Lord, who gave me
my solitude, I watch
the sun descending:
in the marketplace
the stalls empty, the remaining children
bicker at the fountain—
But even at night, when it can't be seen,
the flame of the sun
still heats the pavements.
That's why, on earth,
so much life's sprung up,
because the sun maintains
steady warmth at its periphery.

Does this suggest your meaning:
that the game resumes,
in the dust beneath
the infant god of the fountain;
there is nothing fixed,
there is no assurance of death—

4

I take my basket to the brazen market,
to the gathering place.
I ask you, how much beauty
can a person bear? It is
heavier than ugliness, even the burden
of emptiness is nothing beside it.
Crates of eggs, papaya, sacks of yellow lemons—
I am not a strong woman. It isn't easy
to want so much, to walk
with such a heavy basket, either
bent reed, or willow.

LIBERATION

My mind is clouded,
I cannot hunt anymore.
I lay my gun over the tracks of the rabbit.

It was as though I became that creature
who could not decide
whether to flee or be still
and so was trapped in the pursuer's eyes—

And for the first time I knew
those eyes have to be blank
because it is impossible
to kill and question at the same time.

Then the shutter snapped,
the rabbit went free. He flew
through the empty forest

that part of me
that was the victim.
Only victims have a destiny.

And the hunter, who believed
whatever struggles
begs to be torn apart:

that part is paralyzed.

II

THE EMBRACE

She taught him the gods. Was it teaching? He went on
hating them, but in the long evenings of obsessive talk,
as he listened, they became real. Not that they changed.
They never came to seem innately human.
In the firelight, he watched her face.
But she would not be touched; she had rejected
the original need. Then in the darkness he would lead her
    back—
above the trees, the city rose in a kind of splendor
as all that is wild comes to the surface.

MARATHON

1 LAST LETTER

Weeping, standing still—then going out again into the garden.
In the field, white heads of dandelions making rows of saints,
now bending, now stiff with awe—
and at the edge, a hare: his eyes fixed, terrified.
Silence. Herds of bells—

Without thinking, I knelt in the grass, like someone meaning to
    pray.
When I tried to stand again, I couldn't move,
my legs were utterly rigid. Does grief change you like that?
Through the birches, I could see the pond.
The sun was cutting small white holes in the water.

I got up finally; I walked down to the pond.
I stood there, brushing the grass from my skirt, watching myself,
like a girl after her first lover
turning slowly at the bathroom mirror, naked, looking for a
    sign.
But nakedness in women is always a pose.
I was not transfigured. I would never be free.

2 SONG OF THE RIVER

Once we were happy, we had no memories.
For all the repetition, nothing happened twice.
We were always walking parallel to a river
with no sense of progression
though the trees across from us
were sometimes birch, sometimes cypress—
the sky was blue, a matrix of blue glass.

While, in the river, things were going by—
a few leaves, a child's boat painted red and white,
its sail stained by the water—

As they passed, on the surface we could see ourselves;
we seemed to drift
apart and together, as the river
linked us forever, though up ahead
were other couples, choosing souvenirs.

3 THE ENCOUNTER

You came to the side of the bed
and sat staring at me.
Then you kissed me—I felt
hot wax on my forehead.
I wanted it to leave a mark:
that's how I knew I loved you.
Because I wanted to be burned, stamped,
to have something in the end—
I drew the gown over my head;
a red flush covered my face and shoulders.
It will run its course, the course of fire,
setting a cold coin on the forehead, between the eyes.
You lay beside me; your hand moved over my face
as though you had felt it also—
you must have known, then, how I wanted you.
We will always know that, you and I.
The proof will be my body.

4 SONG OF OBSTACLES

When my lover touches me, what I feel in my body
is like the first movement of a glacier over the earth,
as the ice shifts, dislodging great boulders, hills
of solemn rock: so, in the forests, the uprooted trees
become a sea of disconnected limbs—
And, where there are cities, these dissolve too,
the sighing gardens, all the young girls
eating chocolates in the courtyard, slowly
scattering the colored foil: then, where the city was,
the ore, the unearthed mysteries: so I see
that ice is more powerful than rock, than mere resistance—

Then for us, in its path, time doesn't pass,
not even an hour.

5 NIGHT SONG

Look up into the light of the lantern.
Don't you see? The calm of darkness
is the horror of Heaven.

We've been apart too long, too painfully separated.
How can you bear to dream,
to give up watching? I think you must be dreaming,
your face is full of mild expectancy.

I need to wake you, to remind you that there isn't a future.
That's why we're free. And now some weakness in me
has been cured forever, so I'm not compelled
to close my eyes, to go back, to rectify—

The beach is still; the sea, cleansed of its superfluous life,
opaque, rocklike. In mounds, in vegetal clusters,
seabirds sleep on the jetty. Terns, assassins—

You're tired; I can see that.
We're both tired, we have acted a great drama.
Even our hands are cold, that were like kindling.
Our clothes are scattered on the sand; strangely enough,
they never turned to ashes.

I have to tell you what I've learned, that I know now
what happens to the dreamers.
They don't feel it when they change. One day
they wake, they dress, they are old.

Tonight I'm not afraid
to feel the revolutions. How can you want sleep
when passion gives you that peace?
You're like me tonight, one of the lucky ones.
You'll get what you want. You'll get your oblivion.

6 THE BEGINNING

I had come to a strange city, without belongings:
in the dream, it was your city, I was looking for you.
Then I was lost, on a dark street lined with fruit stands.

There was only one fruit: blood oranges.
The markets made displays of them, beautiful displays—
how else could they compete? And each arrangement had, at its
    center,
one fruit, cut open.

Then I was on a boulevard, in brilliant sunlight.
I was running; it was easy to run, since I had nothing.
In the distance, I could see your house; a woman knelt in the
    yard.
There were roses everywhere; in waves, they climbed the high
    trellis.

Then what began as love for you
became a hunger for structure: I could hear
the woman call to me in common kindness, knowing
I wouldn't ask for you anymore—

So it was settled: I could have a childhood there.
Which came to mean being always alone.

7 FIRST GOODBYE

You can join the others now,
body that wouldn't let my body rest,
go back to the world, to avenues, the ordered
depths of the parks, like great terminals
that never darken: a stranger's waiting for you
in a hundred rooms. Go back to them,
to increment and limitation: near the centered rose,
you watch her peel an orange
so the dyed rind falls in petals on her plate. This
is mastery, whose active
mode is dissection: the enforced light
shines on the blade. Sooner or later
you'll begin to dream of me. I don't envy you
those dreams. I can imagine how my face looks,
burning like that, afflicted with desire—lowered
face of your invention—how the mouth betrays
the isolated greed of the lover
as it magnifies and then destroys:
I don't envy you that visitation.
And the women lying there—who wouldn't pity them,
the way they turn to you, the way
they struggle to be visible. They make
a place for you in bed, a white excavation.
Then the sacrament: your bodies pieced together,
churning, churning, till the heat leaves them entirely—
Sooner or later you will call my name,
cry of loss, mistaken
cry of recognition, of arrested need
for someone who exists in memory: no voice
carries to that kingdom.

Last night I dreamed we were in Venice;
today, we are in Venice. Now, lying here,
I think there are no boundaries to my dreams,
nothing we won't share.
So there is nothing to describe. We're interchangeable
with anyone, in joy
changed to a mute couple.

Then why did we worship clarity,
to speak, in the end, only each other's names,
to speak, as now, not even whole words,
only vowels?

Finally, this is what we craved,
this lying in the bright light without distinction—
we who would leave behind
exact records.

9 MARATHON

I was not meant to hear
the two of them talking.
But I could feel the light of the torch
stop trembling, as though it had been
set on a table. I was not to hear
the one say to the other
how best to arouse me,
with what words, what gestures,
nor to hear the description of my body,
how it responded, what
it would not do. My back was turned.
I studied the voices, soon distinguishing
the first, which was deeper, closer,
from that of the replacement.
For all I know, this happens
every night: somebody waking me, then
the first teaching the second.
What happens afterward
occurs far from the world, at a depth
where only the dream matters
and the bond with any one soul
is meaningless; you throw it away.

SUMMER

Remember the days of our first happiness,
how strong we were, how dazed by passion,
lying all day, then all night in the narrow bed,
sleeping there, eating there too: it was summer,
it seemed everything had ripened
at once. And so hot we lay completely uncovered.
Sometimes the wind rose; a willow brushed the window.

But we were lost in a way, didn't you feel that?
The bed was like a raft; I felt us drifting
far from our natures, toward a place where we'd discover
    nothing.
First the sun, then the moon, in fragments,
shone through the willow.
Things anyone could see.

Then the circles closed. Slowly the nights grew cool;
the pendant leaves of the willow
yellowed and fell. And in each of us began
a deep isolation, though we never spoke of this,
of the absence of regret.
We were artists again, my husband.
We could resume the journey.

III

THE REPROACH

You have betrayed me, Eros.
You have sent me
my true love.

On a high hill you made
his clear gaze;
my heart was not
so hard as your arrow.

What is a poet
without dreams?
I lie awake; I feel
actual flesh upon me,
meaning to silence me—
Outside, in the blackness
over the olive trees,
a few stars.

I think this is a bitter insult:
that I prefer to walk
the coiled paths of the garden,
to walk beside the river
glittering with drops
of mercury. I like to lie
in the wet grass beside the river,
running away, Eros,
not openly, with other men,
but discreetly, coldly—

All my life
I have worshiped the wrong gods.
When I watch the trees
on the other side,
the arrow in my heart
is like one of them,
swaying and quivering.

THE END OF THE WORLD

1 TERRA NOVA

A place without associations—
Where, in the other country, there were mountains
so the mind was made to discover
words for containment, and so on,
here there was water, an extension of the brilliant city.
As for detail: where there had been, before,
nurturing slopes of grass on which, at evening or before rain,
the Charolais would lie, their many eyes
affixed to the traveler, here
there was clay. And yet it blossomed astoundingly:
beside the house, camellia, periwinkle, rosemary in crushing
        profusion—
in his heart, he was a lover again,
calling *now, now,* not restricted
to *once* or *in the old days.* He lay on his back in the wild fennel.
But in fact he was an old man.
Sixty years ago, he took his mother's hand. It was May, his
        birthday.
They were walking in the orchard, in the continuous present,
gathering apple blossoms. Then she wanted him to watch the
        sun;
they had to stand together as it sank in the possessive earth.
How short it seemed, that lifetime of waiting—
this red star blazing over the bay
was all the light of his childhood
that had followed him here.

2 THE TRIBUTE

In that period of strange calm
he wandered down stone steps to the wide harbor:
he was moved; the lights of the city moved him deeply
and it seemed the earth was being offered to him
as a source of awe—he had no wish to change.
He had written, he had built his temple.
So he justified a need to sacrifice.
He leaned against the railing: in the dark bay, he saw the city
        waver;
cells of light floated on the water, they rocked gently, held by
        white threads.
Behind him, on the steps, he heard a man and woman
arguing with great intensity.
In a poem, he could bring them together
like two pieces of a broken toy that could be joined again—
Then the voices ceased, replaced by sighs, rustlings, the little
        sounds
of which he had no knowledge
though the wind persisted
in conveying them to where he stood,
and with them all the odors of summer.

3 THE END OF THE WORLD

It is difficult to describe, coming as it still does
to each person at a different time.
Unique, terrible—and in the sky, uncanny brilliance
substituting for the humanizing sun.
So the blessed kneel, the lucky who expect nothing,
while those who loved the world
are returned by suffering
to what precedes attachment, namely
hatred of pain. Now the bitter are confirmed
in loneliness: they watch the winter sun
mockingly lower itself over the bare earth,
making nothing live—in this light
god approaches the dying.
Not the true god, of course. There is no god
who will save one man.

The Mountain

My students look at me expectantly.
I explain to them that the life of art is a life
of endless labor. Their expressions
hardly change; they need to know
a little more about endless labor.
So I tell them the story of Sisyphus,
how he was doomed to push
a rock up a mountain, knowing nothing
would come of this effort
but that he would repeat it
indefinitely. I tell them
there is joy in this, in the artist's life,
that one eludes
judgment, and as I speak
I am secretly pushing a rock myself,
slyly pushing it up the steep
face of a mountain. Why do I lie
to these children? They aren't listening,
they aren't deceived, their fingers
tapping at the wooden desks—
So I retract
the myth; I tell them it occurs
in hell, and that the artist lies
because he is obsessed with attainment,
that he perceives the summit
as that place where he will live forever,
a place about to be
transformed by his burden: with every breath,
I am standing at the top of the mountain.
Both my hands are free. And the rock has added
height to the mountain.

A PARABLE

It was an epoch of heroes.
So this young boy, this nobody,
making his way from one plain to another,
picks up a small stone among the cold, unspecified
rocks of the hillside. It is a pleasant day.
At his feet, normal vegetation, the few white flowers
like stars, the leaves woolly, sage-green:
at the bottom of the hill are corpses.

Who is the enemy? Who has distributed
the compact bodies of the Jews
in this unprecedented silence? Disguised in dirt,
the scattered army sees the beast, Goliath,
towering above the childish shepherd.
They shut their eyes. And all the level earth
becomes the shattered surface of a sea, so disruptive
is that fall. In the ensuing dust, David
lifts his hand: then it is his, the hushed,
completed kingdom—

Fellow Jews, to plot a hero's journey
is to trace a mountain: hero to god, god to ruler.
At the precipice, the moment we don't want to hear about—
the stone is gone; now
the hand is the weapon.

On the palace roof, King David stares across
the shining city of Jerusalem
into the face of Bathsheba and perceives
his own amplified desire. At heart, he feels nothing.

She is like a flower in a tub of water. Above his head, the clouds move. And it comes to him he has attained all he is capable of dreaming.

DAY WITHOUT NIGHT

The angel of god pushed the child's hand
away from the jewels, toward the burning coal.

I

The image
of truth is fire: it mounts
the fortress of heaven.

Have you never felt
its obvious power?
Even a child
is capable of this joy.

Apparently,
a like sun
burns in hell. It *is* hell,
day without night.

2

It was as though Pharaoh's daughter
had brought home a lion cub
and for a few weeks
passed it off as a cat.
You did not press this woman.
She said she came upon
a child in the rushes;
each time she told the story,
her handmaidens recreated
their interminable chorus of sighs.
It had to be:
A little prince. A little lion cub.

3

And then with almost no encouragement
a sign came: for awhile
the child is like
a grandson to Pharaoh.
Then he squirms; on Pharaoh's lap
he reaches for the crown of Egypt—

4

So Pharaoh set before the child
two trays, one of rubies, one of burning embers:

Light of my heart, the world
is set before you:
fire on either side, fire
without alternative—

5

It was like a magic act: all you saw
was the child move; the same hand that took
such active interest in
the wealth of Egypt showed
this sudden preference for a pile of coal.
You never saw the actual angel.
And to complete the act,
the child maimed himself—
And a cry arose,
almost as though a person
were in hell,
where there is nothing to do
but see—

6

Moses
lay in the rushes:
he could see
only in one direction,
his perspective being
narrowed by the basket.
What he saw
was great light, like
a wing hovering.
And god said to him,
"You can be the favored one,
the one who tastes fire
and cannot speak,
or you can die now
and let the others
stay in Egypt: tell them
it was better to die in Egypt,
better to litter the river
with your corpse, than face
a new world."

7

It was as though a soul emerged,
independent of the angel,
a conscious being choosing
not to enter paradise—
at the same time, the true
sun was setting.
As it touched the water

by necessity the mirrored sun rose
to meet it from
the depths of the river:
Then the cry ended.
Or was hidden
in the stammering
of the redeemer—

    8

The context
of truth is darkness: it sweeps
the deserts of Israel.

Are you taken in
by lights, by illusions?

Here is your path to god,
who has no name, whose hand
is invisible: a trick
of moonlight on the dark water.

ELMS

All day I tried to distinguish
need from desire. Now, in the dark,
I feel only bitter sadness for us,
the builders, the planers of wood,
because I have been looking
steadily at these elms
and seen the process that creates
the writhing, stationary tree
is torment, and have understood
it will make no forms but twisted forms.

ADULT GRIEF

—for E. V.

Because you were foolish enough to love one place,
now you are homeless, an orphan
in a succession of shelters.
You did not prepare yourself sufficiently.
Before your eyes, two people were becoming old;
I could have told you two deaths were coming.
There has never been a parent
kept alive by a child's love.

Now, of course, it's too late—
you were trapped in the romance of fidelity.
You kept going back, clinging
to two people you hardly recognized
after what they'd endured.

If once you could have saved yourself,
now that time's past: you were obstinate, pathetically
blind to change. Now you have nothing:
for you, home is a cemetery.
I've seen you press your face against the granite markers—
you are the lichen, trying to grow there.
But you will not grow,
you will not let yourself
obliterate anything.

HAWK'S SHADOW

Embracing in the road
for some reason I no longer remember
and then drawing apart, seeing
that shape ahead—how close was it?
We looked up to where the hawk
hovered with its kill; I watched them
veering toward West Hill, casting
their one shadow in the dirt, the all-inclusive
shape of the predator—
Then they disappeared. And I thought:
one shadow. Like the one we made,
you holding me.

FROM THE JAPANESE

1

A cat stirs in the material world.
And suddenly sunlight pours into the room
as though somewhere a blind had been opened.
And on the floor, the white bars of a ladder appear.

2

Gwen is sobbing in the front yard; she is three.
The Spanish maid strokes her hair—Gwen
is bilingual; she dries her eyes,
a few petals falling from the jacaranda tree.

Now the door opens: here is Jack, the athlete, in his combat
    boots.
For the next hour he runs
first away from, then toward his family.

And here is Trixie, roaming the driveway,
huge in comparison
to the rigid bird. Boring bird,
that will not chirp and fight anymore.
She flicks it once or twice,
under the grapefruit, under the lemon tree.

Early summer: fog covers the mountains.
Under each tree, a doily of shade.

3

At first, I saw you everywhere.
Now only in certain things,
at longer intervals.

4

We were walking in the Japanese gardens
among the bare cherry trees,
a path you chose
deliberately in desolate November

as though I myself had ordered down
the petals, the black
nuggets of the fruit—

Nearby, a boy sailed his wooden boat,
home and away, home and away.
Then the thread snapped; the boat
was carried toward the waterfall.

"From this moment I will never know
ease," you said, "since you have lied to me,
nor joy." The boy
covered his face with his hands.

There is another world,
neither air nor water
but an emptiness which now
a symbol has entered.

5

The cat
misses her master.
She climbs the brick wall,

a feat
Gwen determines
to copy: loud
objections from the Spanish maid.

Tears, shuffling. At the water's edge,
the boy finally
lowered his hands.
He had a new toy, a thread
tied to a lost thing—

Twilight: in her blue sombrero,
Gwen reconstructs the summer garden.

6

Alone, watching the moon rise:
tonight, a full circle,
like a woman's eye passing over abundance.

This is the most it will ever be.
Above the blank street, the imperfections
solved by night—

Like our hearts: darkness
showed us their capacity.
Our full hearts—at the time, they seemed so impressive.

Cries, moans, our important suffering.
A hand at the small of the back
or on the breast—

And now across the wall
someone is clearing the table,
wrapping the dark bread and the white ceramic pot of butter.

What did we think?
What did we talk about?

Upstairs, a light goes on.
It must be
Gwen's, it burns
the span of a story—

7

Why love what you will lose?
There is nothing else to love.

8

Last night in bed your
hand fell heavily upon
my shoulder. I thought

you slept. Yet we are
parted. Perhaps the sheet moved,
given your hand's weight by

the dampness of
my body. Morning: I have
written to thank you.

9

The cat sleeps on the sidewalk,
black against the white cement.

The brave are patient.
They are the priests of sunrise,
lions on the ramparts, the promontory.

LEGEND

My father's father came
to New York from Dhlua:
one misfortune followed another.
In Hungary, a scholar, a man of property.
Then failure: an immigrant
rolling cigars in a cold basement.

He was like Joseph in Egypt.
At night, he walked the city;
spray of the harbor
turned to tears on his face.

Tears of grief for Dhlua—forty houses,
a few cows grazing the rich meadows—

Though the great soul is said to be
a star, a beacon,
what it resembles better is a diamond:
in the whole world there is nothing
hard enough to change it.

Unfortunate being, have you ceased to feel
the grandeur of the world
that, like a heavy weight, shaped
the soul of my grandfather?

From the factory, like sad birds his dreams
flew to Dhlua, grasping in their beaks
as from moist earth in which a man could see
the shape of his own footprint,

scattered images, loose bits of the village;
and as he packed the leaves, so within his soul
this weight compressed scraps of Dhlua
into principles, abstractions
worthy of the challenge of bondage:

in such a world, to scorn
privilege, to love
reason and justice, always
to speak the truth—

which has been
the salvation of our people
since to speak the truth gives
the illusion of freedom.

MORNING

The virtuous girl wakes in the arms of her husband,
the same arms in which, all summer, she moved
restlessly, under the pear trees:
it is pleasant to wake like this,
with the sun rising, to see the wedding dress
draped over the back of a chair,
and on the heavy bureau, a man's shirt, neatly folded;
to be restored by these
to a thousand images, to the church itself, the autumn sunlight
streaming through the colored windows, through
the figure of the Blessed Virgin, and underneath,
Amelia holding the fiery bridal flowers—
As for her mother's tears: ridiculous, and yet
mothers weep at their daughters' weddings,
everyone knows that, though
for whose youth one cannot say.
At the great feast there is always the outsider, the stranger to joy
and the point is how different they are, she and her mother.
Never has she been further from sadness
than she is now. She feels no call to weep,
but neither does she know
the meaning of that word, youth.

HORSE

What does the horse give you
that I cannot give you?

I watch you when you are alone,
when you ride into the field behind the dairy,
your hands buried in the mare's
dark mane.

Then I know what lies behind your silence:
scorn, hatred of me, of marriage. Still,
you want me to touch you; you cry out
as brides cry, but when I look at you I see
there are no children in your body.
Then what is there?

Nothing, I think. Only haste
to die before I die.

In a dream, I watched you ride the horse
over the dry fields and then
dismount: you two walked together;
in the dark, you had no shadows.
But I felt them coming toward me
since at night they go anywhere,
they are their own masters.

Look at me. You think I don't understand?
What is the animal
if not passage out of this life?

Index of Poems

INDEX

A

Abishag, 87
Adult Grief. 202
All Hallows, 61
Aphrodite, 141
Apple Trees, The, 99
Archipelago, 65
Aubade, 140
Autumnal, 139

B

Baskets, 169
Brennende Liebe, 86
Bridal Piece, 26
Brooding Likeness, 159

C

Cell, The, 34
Chicago Train, The, 5
Cottonmouth Country, 43
Cripple in the Subway, The, 30

D

Day Without Night, 197
Dedication to Hunger, 130
Departure, 79
Descending Figure, 113
Dream of Mourning, The, 143
Drowned Children, The, 105

E

Early December in Croton-on-
   Hudson, 17
Easter Season, 46
Edge, The, 21
Egg, The, 6
Elms, 201
Embrace, The, 175
End of the World, The, 191
Epithalamium, 119

Exile, 160

F

Fire, The, 92
Firstborn, 38
Flowering Plum, 70
For My Mother, 64
For Jane Myers, 74
Fortress, The, 93
From the Japanese, 204

G

Game, The, 40
Garden, The, 106
Gemini, 80
Gift, The, 144
Grandmother in the Garden, 22
Gratitude, 75
Gretel in Darkness, 63

H

Happiness, 135
Hawk's Shadow, 203
Here Are My Black Clothes, 94
Hestitate to Call, 10
Horse, 212
Hyacinth, 166

I

Illuminations, 120
Inlet, The, 54
Islander, The, 35

J

Japonica, 98
Jeanne d'Arc, 78

L

La Force, 39
Labor Day, 13

Lady in the Single, The, 29
Lamentations, 147
Late Snow, 50
Legend, 209
Letter from Provence, 36
Letter from Our Man in
    Blossomtime, 33
Letters, The, 97
Liberation, 172
Love Poem, 90

M
Magi, The, 66
Marathon, 176
Memo from the Cave, 37
Meridian, 49
Messengers, 68
Metamorphosis, 156
Mirror, The, 121
Mock Orange, 155
Morning, 211
Mountain, The, 194
Murderess, The, 69
My Cousin in April, 11
My Neighbor in the Mirror, 27
My Life before Dawn, 28
Mythic Fragment, 165

N
Nativity Poem, 71
Night Piece, 127
Northwood Path, 91
Nurse's Song, 31

P
Palais des Arts, 111
Parable, A, 195
Phenomenal Survivals of Death
    in Nantucket, 44
Pictures of the People in the
    War, 23
Pietà, 112
Poem, 76
Pomegranate, 84
Pond, The, 62
Porcelain Bowl, 129

Portland, 1968, 128
Portrait, 122
Portrait of the Queen in Tears,
    25

R
Racer's Widow, The, 24
Reproach, The, 189
Return, The, 146
Returning a Lost Child, 12
Rosy, 142

S
Saturnalia, 55
School Children, The, 77
Scraps, 47
Seated Figure, 164
Seconds, 32
Shad-blow Tree, The, 67
Silverpoint, 16
Slave Ship, The, 52
Solstice, 53
Still Life, 73
Summer, 186
Swans, 126
Swimmer, The, 96

T
Tango, 123
Thanksgiving (from *Firstborn*), 9
Thanksgiving (from *Descending
    Figure*), 116
To Florida, 51
To Autumn, 72
Tree House, The, 48
Triumph of Achilles, The, 168
12.6.71, 89

U
Under Taurus, 95
Undertaking, The, 83

W
Winter Morning, 161
World Breaking Apart, 145
Wound, The, 14